Presented to

_____

By

_____

On

_____

LASS

A story for children based on the best-selling book

Lessons from a Sheep Dog

by Phillip Keller

Roland Gebauer
Illustrated by Cheri Bladholm

Tommy
NELSON

Thomas Nelson, Inc.

Nashville

This book is dedicated to Phillip Keller,
whom our Heavenly Father has used
to deeply influence my life.

The author wishes to thank Mr. Phillip Keller, who graciously gave permission and encouragement to write a children's version of his work, *Lessons from a Sheep Dog.* Special appreciation goes to my wife Hanni, family members, and friends for their meticulous comments and corrections. Working with Laura Minchew and Beverly Phillips of Tommy Nelson™ has been a delightful experience.

Managing Editor: Laura Minchew
Project Editor: Beverly Phillips
Interior Design: Debbie Eicholtz

Library of Congress Cataloging-in-Publication Data
Gebauer, Roland, 1937–
    Lass / Roland Gebauer ; illustrated by Cheri Bladholm.
        p. cm.
    "A story for children based on the best-selling book 'Lessons from a sheep dog' by Phillip Keller."
    Summary: Mr. Keller adopts a sheepdog, Lass, and persuades her to trust and love him, just as he has come to trust and love God.
    ISBN 0-8499-1499-3
    [1. Dogs—Non-Fiction. 2. Christian life—Non-Fiction.] I. Bladholm, Cheri, ill. II. Keller, W. Phillip (Weldon Phillip), 1920–   Lessons from a sheep dog. III. Title
PZ7.G2553Las 1997
[Fic]—dc21
                                                                        97-9997
                                                                        CIP
                                                                        AC

Printed in the United States of America

97 98 99 00 01 02 RRD 9 8 7 6 5 4 3 2 1

A Note about Lass

She was a magnificent Border collie, a dog of unusual intelligence and extraordinary loyalty. It was through our companionship and shared work that Our Father showed me clearly how He longed for my undivided devotion to Himself.

Those lessons, learned so long ago, on my wild acres by the sea, have been shared with multitudes both in the book as well as in the film, and video entitled *Lessons from a Sheep Dog*. Christ Himself has used them to touch and inspire many lives.

Now the touching story of Lass has been retold, once more, especially for children and those who read to them. It is a noble endeavor by Roland Gebauer to reach those with malleable minds and gentle souls. May our Father use this work in His own wonderful way to draw many to Himself, in loving loyalty and quiet trust.

W. Phillip Keller

W. Phillip Keller
April 1996

Contents

Notes to Parents, Grandparents, and Other Readers

Reading aloud to our five children over the years has been a wonderful bridge into their hearts and minds. There are few thrills in life that rival the concentrated gaze in the eyes of a child absorbed in a story expressively presented by an understanding adult.

Lass is intended to be read aloud to children ages five and up. For the younger ones, reading one chapter at a time might be appropriate. Not only does the story transmit realistic experiences of working with sheep and sheep dogs, but it also explores spiritual applications. Questions and sample applications are listed at the end of each chapter.

Don't be too quick to provide pat answers. Allow your children to come up with their own questions and answers suited to their level. You'll find that they are quite perceptive and capable of drawing their own conclusions when presented with valid information.

At the end of the book you will find additional suggestions for guided discussions with children. What a great opportunity to expand your child's understanding of God our Father, Creator of the universe, and Jesus Christ our Good Shepherd.

—Roland Gebauer

1

Trouble at Fairwinds

Many years ago, on Vancouver Island, there was a beautiful ranch called Fairwinds. A young man named Phillip Keller lived on the ranch. He wanted to raise sheep, but he had a problem. "Paddy," the big cattle dog he had brought with him to Fairwinds, didn't know one thing about sheep. Paddy wasn't even interested in sheep. The dog just lay around in the sun or slept by the fire.

One day Mr. Keller said, "If I'm going to raise sheep, I will need a dog that has been trained to handle sheep."

Soon after that, Mr. Keller saw an ad in the newspaper:

```
Wanted: A good country home for pure-bred
Border collie. Chases cars and bicycles.
```

Mr. Keller quickly phoned the owner. He set up a time to see the dog.

Early the next day Mr. Keller started up his old car and drove to town. The lady who owned the dog was waiting for him.

"Mr. Keller," she said, "I hope you can do something with Lassie. She is absolutely crazy. All she does is chase cars and children on bicycles. She jumps all the fences and upsets the neighbors. She is too wild to live in town."

As they rounded the corner of the house, a bundle of dirty black fur jumped toward them, growling loudly. A heavy chain around the dog's neck jerked her back. She dropped into a heap on the ground. Her ears were laid back in anger. Deep mean growls rumbled in her throat.

When Mr. Keller took a closer look at the snarling animal, he felt a great sadness. There was another chain from the dog's right hind leg to her collar.

Yet through all the angry growling and dirt, Mr. Keller saw that Lassie had all the traits of a good sheep dog. She had a broad chest, strong legs, and intelligent eyes.

"How old is Lassie?" Mr. Keller asked.

"She is two years old and crazy," the owner answered. "She was such a good little puppy when I got her. I don't know what went wrong with her. Nobody wants her. I have to keep her chained to her doghouse all the time. If you don't take her, she'll have to be put to sleep."

Mr. Keller was sure he knew what went wrong. *Lassie is in the wrong hands and the wrong place*, he thought to himself. *Lassie is a Border collie, a sheep dog. She needs room to run. She needs to handle sheep. Border collies are very smart. They can work long hours without tiring, and they're loyal. What a shame! This wonderful animal has everything she needs to be a good sheep dog, but she doesn't know it. She's been treated like a failure.*

Mr. Keller could sense the frustration in Lassie and longed to set her free to do what she was bred for—handling sheep.

Mr. Keller turned to the lady and said, "By the time dogs are two years old, they usually have learned all they will ever learn. Lassie, here, is really too old. But I would like to give her a chance. I will make a deal with you. If she doesn't respond to me after six weeks, I will bring her back, and you can do what needs to be done." The lady gladly agreed.

Carefully Mr. Keller removed the heavy chain and placed a new, soft collar around Lassie's neck. She cringed and growled every time his hands touched her. As they were driving back to the ranch, Mr. Keller spoke in a soft, low voice to the dog.

"Now that you are starting a new life, I'm going to give you a new name. How does Lass sound to you? It goes well with your Scottish blood." Mr. Keller knew that the Border collie breed had first started in the border region between England and Scotland.

He reached behind him to where Lass lay. He tried to pet her, but she only growled and showed her teeth. "It will take time to win the trust of this poor dog," Mr. Keller said to himself.

Back at Fairwinds, Mr. Keller fastened Lass's soft leash near the new doghouse. Mrs. Keller had a bowl of delicious food and fresh, clean water waiting for the new dog. But Lass would not touch any of it. She just stared at them in anger.

Day after day she refused to eat or drink. Soon she began to lose weight. After a week, Mr. Keller said to his wife, "I'm going to take Lass off the leash and set her free to prove that I trust her. She won't be forced. She has to come to us because she chooses to."

As soon as the leash was removed, Lass took off like a flash and disappeared into the forest. Anxiously the Kellers waited for Lass to return. After several days, Mr. Keller checked with other ranchers in the neighborhood, but no one had seen the dog. He searched up and down the country roads, but he didn't find her. Lass seemed to have disappeared into the salty ocean air. Sadly Mr. Keller returned to the ranch. He wondered, *What now? Who would help him raise his sheep?*

Why did Lass run off when her leash was removed?

APPLICATION: Lass had been mistreated for so long, that she didn't expect kindness. She expected Mr. Keller to treat her just as her first owner had. You know, sometimes when people learn about Jesus for the first time, they don't trust Him. They can't believe that He is not like people who have hurt them or treated them badly. But just like Mr. Keller wanted to take care of Lass, Jesus wants to take good care of us.

2

Hopeful Signs

*O*ne evening Mr. Keller was busy in the yard. He noticed something moving on top of the large rocks behind the house. There was Lass, crouching like a cougar, staring down at him. But she still was not ready to trust her new owner.

When Mr. Keller called her name, she turned and fled back into the forest. He felt sorry for her. *Maybe, if I place some food up on the rocks, she'll understand that I love her,* Mr. Keller thought.

Every evening he took food and water up to the rock. When he checked in the morning, they were gone. As Lass ate the food, she began to gain weight. But still she would have nothing to do with Mr. Keller.

As the weeks went by, Lass came to the rocks more often. One day, some ewes with their lambs were grazing near her lookout. Suddenly Lass sat up on her hind legs. She tilted her head and watched the sheep very closely.

Are her instincts finally coming alive? Mr. Keller wondered hopefully. He felt sorry for Lass. He really wanted to become friends with her. Every evening Mr. Keller began to take a few sheep to graze near the dog's lookout. He hoped that Lass would get interested in them. But she stayed away.

Many days passed. The time was nearing when Mr. Keller would have to take Lass back to her previous owner to be put to sleep, unless the dog began to respond.

Then, one quiet evening, Mr. Keller was watching his sheep near the shore. A gentle breeze floated up from the water. While the sheep peacefully munched grass, Mr. Keller enjoyed the colorful sunset.

Suddenly, without warning, Mr. Keller felt a soft, warm nose touching his hand. His heart almost skipped a beat. Was it possible? He could barely look for fear of driving Lass away again. She had finally come by her own choosing. She was finally responding to all the love and attention he had shown her. She had found the courage to make a new start, to put her trust in a new master.

Lass was content to let him pet her gently. Mr. Keller was very happy. His heart was bursting with joy. A friendship had begun. Everything would turn out all right

---

Why did Lass start to trust Mr. Keller?

APPLICATION: Lass finally understood that she could trust Mr. Keller. She was ready to make a new start. God gives us the choice to come to Him, or to live without Him. Yet, God wants very much for us to trust Him. He can help us to be the special person He made us to be. God wants to do great things with our lives. But first, we have to trust in Him.

3

Learning the Trade

Soon Lass learned to trust her new master. She let him clean and brush her fur. She learned that Mr. Keller loved and understood her and wanted what was best for her. She learned to obey commands, such as "Come"—"Lie down"—"Sit"—"Fetch them"—"Stay"—"To the left"—"To the right." Lass was always eager to please Mr. Keller.

She would look at her master with her big, brown eyes, waiting for his commands. When Lass obeyed his commands, Mr. Keller would pat her head and stroke her shiny black fur. In return, Lass would give Mr. Keller a sloppy kiss and happy yelp. Then, she would run around him in big circles.

Seeing how much Lass loved and respected him, Mr. Keller thought about his own life. He thought about the many times God had come to him in love. At first Mr. Keller had pulled back.

Then, one day, he trusted Jesus and gave Him complete control over his life. How wonderfully Mr. Keller's life had changed. It was scary to think what would have happened to him if he had not trusted God. What would have happened to Lass if she had not overcome her fears and trusted Mr. Keller?

Sometimes a sheep dog is far away from the shepherd when working the sheep. When this happens the sheep dog must obey his master's silent hand signals. Lass learned to watch for Mr. Keller's arm and hand signals. She developed great skill in handling the sheep. Many people heard about the amazing work Lass did. Strangers would drive out from the city just to see Mr. Keller and his beautiful Border collie round up the sheep.

As their friendship grew, Lass became a "one-man dog." She was totally devoted to her master. In the beginning she had been so shy, afraid, and angry. But now, like a shadow, Lass followed Mr. Keller around wherever he went. She was happy with no one else. Only Mr. Keller could feed her. If he left the ranch for some reason, she would not eat or drink until he came back.

Lass was doing what she was created for, handling sheep, and she loved it. She did her work with great energy. Because Lass had learned to obey and trust her master, she was becoming a great sheep dog.

Why was it important for Lass to obey Mr. Keller?

APPLICATION: Isn't it wonderful that God knows everything about us? He loves us very much. He sent His Son, Jesus, who forgives us when we make bad choices. Just like Mr. Keller washed and cleaned Lass, Jesus cleans the ugliness in our hearts with His forgiveness when we ask Him. Then, He makes us want to do what is right. We are happiest when we love and obey Jesus because that's what we were created to do.

4

The Hardest Lesson

At Mr. Keller's Fairwinds ranch, Lass was learning her lessons well. But there was one command that she had a hard time following. It was the signal "Stay." Sometimes it meant that she was to hold a group of little lambs in the corner of a field. Sometimes she had to keep rams on the loading ramp while Mr. Keller was busy doing something else. Lass always wanted to be where the action was. It was very hard for her to stay in one place. Always tempted to leave her post, she would sometimes "break faith" and take off, leaving the sheep unattended.

Two things caused Lass to want to disobey her master's orders to stay—crows and sparks.

One day Mr. Keller and Lass were in the middle of moving the loudly bleating flock of sheep. Suddenly, several black crows came flying over the fields. Swooping down low over Lass, the noisy black birds teased the sheep dog with their loud cries. The birds dived from the air, flying just above Lass's head. The wind whistled over their wings.

Unable to hold herself back, Lass raced away after the crows. Her graceful body seemed to fly over the field. She was having great fun. After a while she gave up and came back. Lass was very tired, her tongue hung from her mouth. She looked up into Mr. Keller's face and turned her head to one side, as if to say, "What a great sport that was. I really scared them away! I hope you are pleased with me."

Yes, she had put on an amazing show, but it had not been good for the sheep or her master. The sheep were all out of order. It would take extra time to get them all together again.

In the fall, the ranchers cleared their land by burning brush, deadwood, and old stumps. The huge fires sent flaming sparks high into the air. The wind carried the glowing sparks some distance.

Lass had never seen such fireworks. Forgetting her duties, she went leaping and bounding after these flying sparks. Some of the sparks got caught in her silky fur, causing it to burn. To put out her burning fur, Lass rolled wildly in the grass. Then, shaking herself, she came racing back as if to say, "Well, boss, wasn't that a great show?"

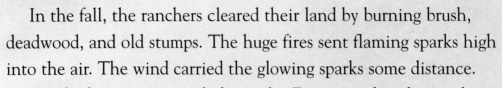

Mr. Keller wasn't pleased with Lass. She had "broken faith," forgotten the sheep, and wasted her energies.

Lass always knew when Mr. Keller was disappointed. She felt guilty for her bad behavior. She hung her head in shame when Mr. Keller scolded her about disobeying.

Mr. Keller didn't enjoy disciplining Lass, it was a difficult time for both of them, but it had to be done. Lass had to be corrected so that next time she would remember to stay with the sheep. The well-being of the flock and the success of the ranch depended on Lass obeying Mr. Keller.

31

When the discipline was over, Mr. Keller gave Lass a big hug, petted her head, and whispered in her ear, "It's all over, girl!" Then her eyes sparkled again. She would shake with joy. With pure pleasure she would race through the grass in a wide circle. Then she'd come running back for another hug. It was her way of showing how much she loved her master.

Why was it important for Mr. Keller to discipline Lass?

APPLICATION: God wants us to have fun, but He also wants us to obey. Mr. Keller didn't mind if Lass ran and played when she didn't have an important job to do. But when he told her to stay and she didn't, Lass was not obeying her master. When your mom or dad asks you to put away your things, you have a choice. You can obey by doing what they ask, or you can do something else and not obey. God is very pleased when we obey. God still loves us, but it makes Him sad when we disobey.

5

Danger on the Range

Life at Mr. Keller's Fairwinds ranch wasn't always peaceful. In the wild open country behind the ranch, there were some stray dogs and cougars. Sheep ranchers always had to be on the lookout for these animals and other things that might harm their flocks.

Mr. Keller had also heard of rustlers, people who steal sheep. They would drive right up to a fence and cut the wires to make a wide opening. Then they would send their trained dogs into the pasture to steal a bunch of sheep. The dogs would lead the sheep right into the truck to be taken away.

To protect his flock, Mr. Keller hung small copper bells around the necks of some of his sheep. This would alert Mr. Keller to problems. When the sheep were grazing happily, the bells made a soft musical tinkling sound. When the sheep were surprised or disturbed, they would begin to run with their bells clanging wildly.

One dark night Mr. Keller was awakened by the alarmed jangling of sheep bells. He jumped out of bed, grabbed his flashlight and his rifle, and dashed out into the fields. What had upset the sheep? Were they being scared by dogs, cougars, or rustlers?

Lass was by his side instantly. There was no need to call her. She knew what was up. Mr. Keller's thoughts went back to other nighttime adventures. He was always amazed how Lass seemed to love all of this excitement. Not once had she cringed in fear. Not once had she decided she would rather stay in the warm comfort of her doghouse.

Lass leaped up in the dark and licked Mr. Keller's hand. It was as if to say, "Cheer up, master, this is a great adventure!"

So, off they went side by side to see what the trouble was. There was real danger for Lass and Mr. Keller. Rustlers had been known to shoot a rancher's dog the minute they saw it. Stray dogs sometimes ganged up on the sheep dog.

There had also been times at Fairwinds when a cougar had attacked the flock during the night. When Mr. Keller checked his flock the next morning, he sometimes discovered dead sheep lying in the fields.

Mr. Keller thought of all these things as he and Lass hurried to their flock. When they reached the sheep, they sat down quietly, looking for the problem. Mr. Keller had his rifle over his knees, ready for action. Lass lay crouched beside him. Her eyes never closed, and her ears were alert to every sound. A deep growl rumbled in the sheep dog's chest every time something caught her attention. Each time, Mr. Keller tightened his grip on the rifle to be ready if needed.

With Lass's keen sense of smell and hearing, Mr. Keller was sure that even a prowling cougar couldn't surprise them in the dark.

Then it happened. The loud, horrible screech of a hunting cougar shattered the silence. A dark shadow flung itself from the big rocks near the sheep. Mr. Keller didn't wait to get the rifle to his shoulder. He fired from the hip at the fast moving cougar.

As suddenly as it had appeared, the wild, fierce cat disappeared into the night.

With his heart still racing, Mr. Keller tried to calm the nervous sheep with soothing words. When they recognized Mr. Keller and Lass, the sheep knew that their shepherd and his dog had come to protect them. In a few moments the flock settled down for the night, quietly chewing the cud.

Why wasn't Lass or Mr. Keller afraid?

APPLICATION: Lass wasn't afraid of danger. Walking next to Mr. Keller, she knew her master would protect her and keep her safe. In the same way, Mr. Keller knew that his Heavenly Father would protect him. God knows what danger is around us. We can trust in Him.

6

A Trusted Companion

Lass became a valuable worker on the Fairwinds ranch. She was so good at handling the flock, she was worth several hired men to Mr. Keller. Lass was always willing to do anything her master asked of her. Sometimes the job was unpleasant. Fairwinds had some pretty tough terrain. Tangled shrubs and prickly rose bushes grew among big rocks and fallen trees. The sheep would scatter all over this rough country searching for special, sweet mouthfuls of grass and leaves.

Mr. Keller always counted his sheep. He knew when some were missing. He was also tall and could see the stragglers half hidden behind brush and big rocks. Because Lass was short, she could not always see these sheep. When Mr. Keller sent Lass into these tough spots to round up the stragglers, Lass had to go in "blind." She had to trust her master completely.

"Bring them in, Lass, bring them in!" Mr. Keller commanded. "Don't leave a single sheep behind."

Upon hearing her master's words, Lass would go bounding away over the rocks, through the brush, into the rose thickets. She never thought about herself. When she finally came out with all the flock, Lass's face would be scratched, her fur clogged with burs, and her paws torn. Lass was obedient. She never minded the pain and bother of the job she had been asked to do.

Mr. Keller was delighted by the dog's unquestioning loyalty. It reminded him of how Jesus, his Good Shepherd, wanted him to be His helper in this world. Mr. Keller asked himself, "Am I willing to go where the Lord sends me, no matter how hard it seems? Am I as happy and eager as Lass to carry out God's wishes?"

And so, with the help of Lass, Fairwinds became a thriving sheep ranch. Mr. Keller learned many lessons from his faithful friend, Lass, the amazing sheep dog.

Why was it important for Lass to bring in the lost sheep?

APPLICATION: Jesus wants us to love others as He has loved us. If we make up our minds to do what He shows us to do, then He will use us to help many people get to know Him better.

Suggestions for Guided Discussions with Children

The following discussion guide is designed to help adults
lead children into a deeper understanding of God's love for them
and how they can respond to that love. By seeing how Lass learned
to trust Mr. Keller, it will be easier for children to understand the
concept of trusting in God's love. To guide them in this discussion,
ask questions that will cover the following points.

Chapter One—Trouble at Fairwinds

Main idea: *Learning about God's care.*

1. Lass was unhappy at her first home. How have other people made you sad or unhappy?

2. How do you know you can trust God?

3. Talk about ways God takes care of us.

Chapter Two—Hopeful Signs

Main idea: *Learning to trust.*

1. Mr. Keller didn't force Lass to trust him. Neither does God force us to trust Him. Why?

2. How did Lass show she had learned to trust Mr. Keller?

3. How do we show God we trust Him?

Chapter Three—Learning the Trade

Main idea: *Learning to obey.*

1. Lass learned to understand and obey Mr. Keller's hand signals. What does God use to speak to us?

2. Name some of the things God tells us to do in His Word, the Bible.

3. What do you think Jesus would like you to do?

Chapter Four—The Hardest Lesson

Main idea: *Facing temptation.*

1. How did Lass disobey Mr. Keller?

2. Crows and sparks were Lass's greatest temptations. What things keep you from obeying God, your parents, or teachers?

3. How does God feel when we do not obey His Word?

Chapter Five—Danger on the Range

Main idea: *Facing danger.*

1. What did Mr. Keller do so he would know when his sheep were in trouble?

2. Why wasn't Lass afraid when she walked next to Mr. Keller to find out what had frightened the sheep?

3. In what ways does God protect us from things or people who try to hurt us?

Chapter Six—A Trusted Companion

Main idea: *Sharing God's love with others.*

1. Lass was always happy and eager to do what Mr. Keller asked her to do. Why should we always be happy to do what God asks us to do?

2. In what ways can we teach our friends about God's love and friendship?

3. Read together John 15:9–14 from the Bible. Then write a poem or a story, or draw a picture about ways we can love one another.